IDLES

×

Magda Archer

Brutalism

Illustrated Lyrics

TEENY TINY WEE LITTLE FLUFFY DUCKIE

IDLES

×

Magda Archer

Brutalism

Illustrated Lyrics

Lyrics by Joe Talbot
Artwork by Magda Archer

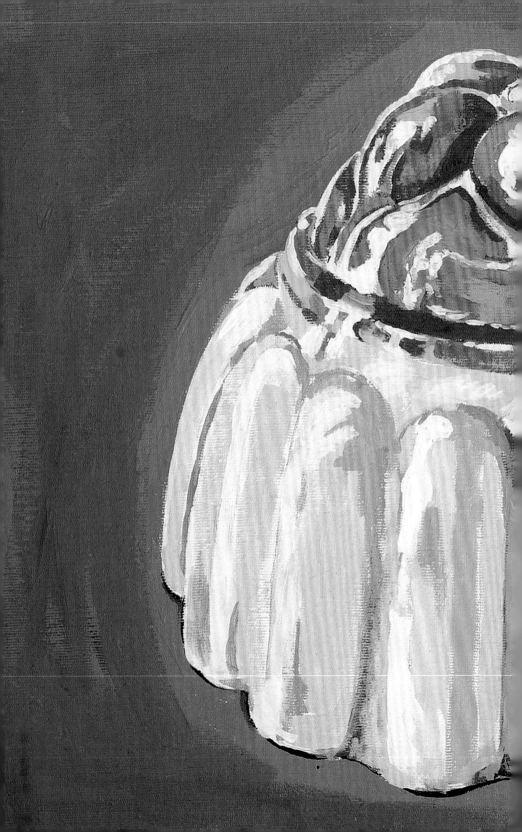

On reflection, I think *Brutalism* saved my life. I was wading in decay and had a severe chip on my shoulder. Nothing and everything was my fault. Drugs were a crutch and a weapon. My ma's slow death was an excuse to be a prick and a push to be a better person. I was a scared wee boy in an unwanted man's body. I was full of love but projecting fear. This balance of imbalance was a real tapestry of fuckery but one that I knew deep deep down was a beautiful thing. I have grown to know just how lucky I am and was during *Brutalism*; not only for my people carrying me but for the fortune of fortitude. We were blindly willing to keep going no matter what. We would not stop to check on peers nor for air. It was a last-chance-saloon bosh and we were laughing into the fire, fearless and afraid. Young in the world and old to our industry, we had seemingly nothing to lose. At a time of death and dying, it was a beautiful time to be alive.

All contradictions in British culture are opportunities to laugh at the terrifying irony of existence and a class system that has absolutely no place in humanity except for the gain of the bloated few. I knew that my humour was that of fitting contortion in a time of either laugh or cry. Laugh or cry, we made and will make as long as our eyes, ears and hands will allow. I knew that then and I know it now. So does Magda Archer. I've been a fan of Magda's work for a long while and it was a real privilege to have the opportunity to ask of her. Magda obliged, wielding her wit and vulnerability with charm and vice. It's something I have strived to achieve myself and not grasped as she has; the essence and cathartic purity from a poised and honest brush stroke that needs no further explanation. Maybe it's grace? Maybe it's emotional maturity? Whatever it is, I am grateful for the journey and I am grateful for Magda.

Fuck the king.

Love,
Joe

Heel /

Heal

01

I want to move into a Bovis home
And make a list of everything I own
And ride into the amber setting sun
Marching to the beat of someone's drum

I'm done

I want to move into a Bovis home
And make a list of everything I own
And ride into the amber setting sun
Marching to the beat of someone's drum

I'm done
What fun
I'm done

(I'm not saying that I'm not like you)
(I'm just saying that I don't like you)
(I'm not saying that I'm not like you)
(I'm just saying that I don't like you)
(I'm not saying that I'm not like you)
(I'm just saying that I don't like you)

I want to move into a Bovis home
And make a list of everything I own
And ride into the amber setting sun
Marching to the beat of someone's drum

I'm done
What fun
I'm done

(I'm not saying that I'm not like you)
(I'm just saying that I don't like you)
(I'm not saying that I'm not like you)
(I'm just saying that I don't like you)
(I'm not saying that I'm not like you)
(I'm just saying that I don't like you)

I want to move into a Bovis home
And make a list of everything I own
And ride into the amber setting sun
Marching to the beat of someone's drum

(I'm not saying that I'm not like you)
(I'm just saying that I don't like you)
(I'm not saying that I'm not like you)
(I'm just saying that I don't like you)
(I'm not saying that I'm not like you)
(I'm just saying that I don't like you)

Ahhhhh
Ahhhh
What fun

I want to move into a Bovis home
And make a list of everything I own
And ride into the amber setting sun
Marching to the beat of someone's drum

(I'm not saying that I'm not like you)
(I'm just saying that I don't like you)
(I'm not saying that I'm not like you)
(I'm just saying that I don't like you)
I'm not saying that I'm not like you)
I'm just saying that I don't like you)

I'm done
What fun
I'm fun

Heel,
Heal
Heel,
Heal
Heel,
Heal
Heel,
Heal
ee
ee

IDLES × Magda Archer

Well

Done

02

WELL DONE

Why don't you get a job?
Even Tarquin has a job
Mary Berry's got a job
So why don't you get a job?

WELL DONE

Why don't you win a medal?
Even Tarquin wins a medal
Mary Berry's got a medal
So why don't you get a medal?

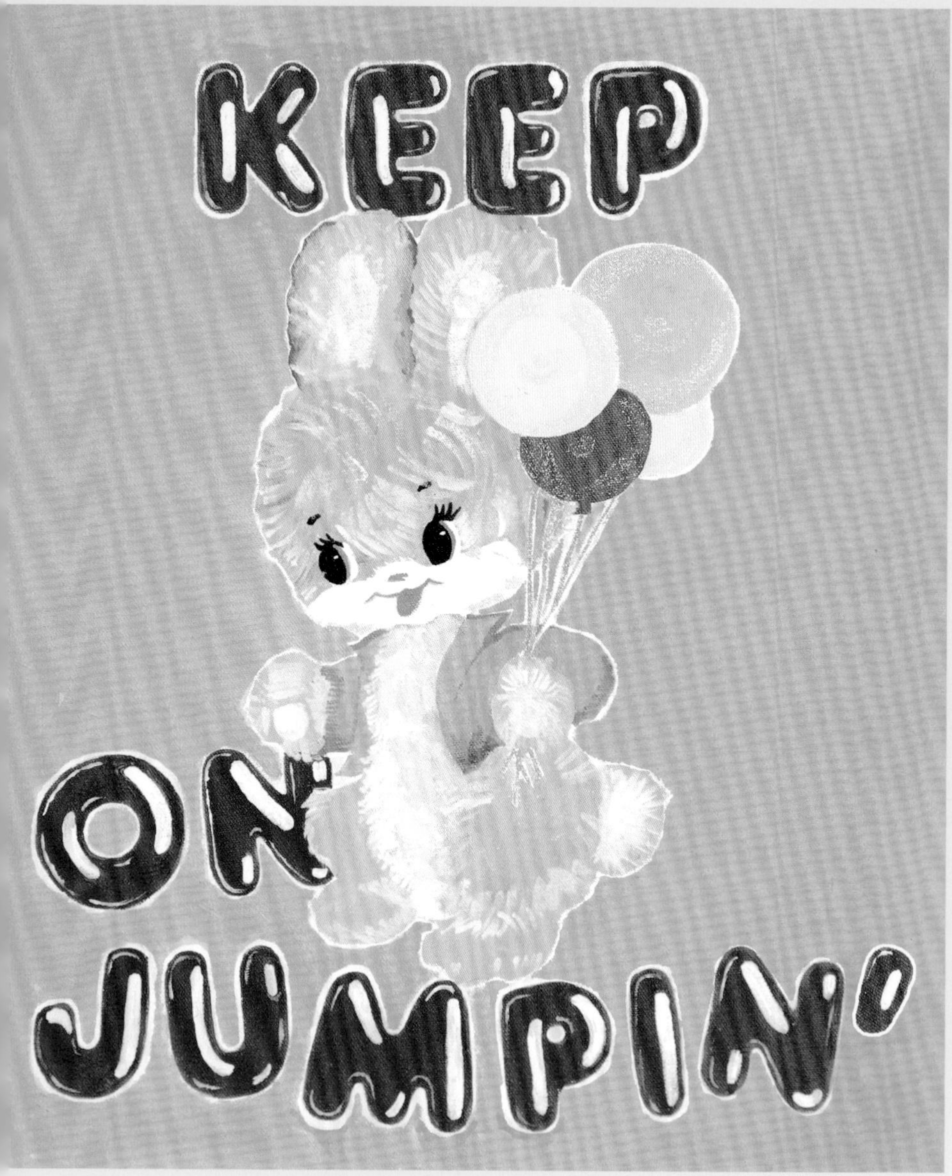
KEEP
ON
JUMPIN'

WELL DONE

I'd rather cut my nose off
To spite my face
I'd rather bite my nose off
To spite my face

Why don't you get a degree?
Even Tarquin has a degree
Mary Berry's got a degree
So why don't you get a degree?

WELL DONE

Why don't you like reggae?
Even Tarquin likes reggae
Mary Berry loves reggae
So why don't you like reggae?

WELL DONE

Why don't you watch football?
Even Tarquin likes football
Trevor Nelson likes football
So why don't you watch football?

WELL DONE

I'd rather cut my nose off
To spite my face
I'd rather bite my nose off
To spite my ...

Ahh! ...

'Get on your bike!'
she said
'Let them eat cake!'
she said

NELL DONE

Ahh! ...

I'd rather bite my nose off
To spite my face
I'd rather bite my nose off
To spite my face

IDLES × Magda Archer

Mother

03

My mother
worked
fifteen hours
five days a week
My mother
worked
sixteen hours
six days a week
My mother
worked
seventeen hours
seven days
a week

The best way to

scare a Tory is to

read and get rich

The best way to

scare a Tory is to

read and get rich

The best way to

scare a Tory is to

read and get rich

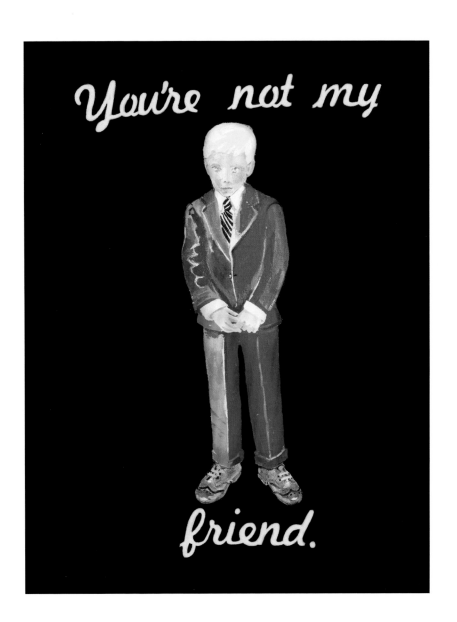

I
know
nothing

I'm just

sitting
here

colours

looking
at

pretty

Mother

Fucker

Mother

Fucker

My mother
worked
fifteen hours
five days a week
My mother
worked
sixteen hours
six days a week
My mother
worked
seventeen hours
seven days
a week

The best way to

scare a Tory is to

read and get rich

The best way to

scare a Tory is to

read and get rich

The best way to

scare a Tory is to

read and get rich

I
know
nothing Mother

should

you

Fucker

looking

I'm just at

sitting

Mother here

pretty

Fucker

Sexual violence doesn't

Mother

start and end with rape

It starts in our books and

Fucker

behind our school gates

Men are scared women

Mother

will laugh in their face

Whereas women are scared

Fucker

it's their lives men will take

IDLES × Magda Archer

Date

Night

04

Date night Date night

PATIENCE
I've got no goddamn patience
But I tried to shake shake shake it up
But I shook myself to boredom

BEST FRIEND
I do not like your best friend
And all those shades of grey–AH
They turn my blood so cold cold cold cold!

When it comes around
We barely scream or shout
Or rarely am I there
And neither of us care

'Cause I, I, I, I, I guess we was born to fail I, I, I, I, I guess we was born to fail

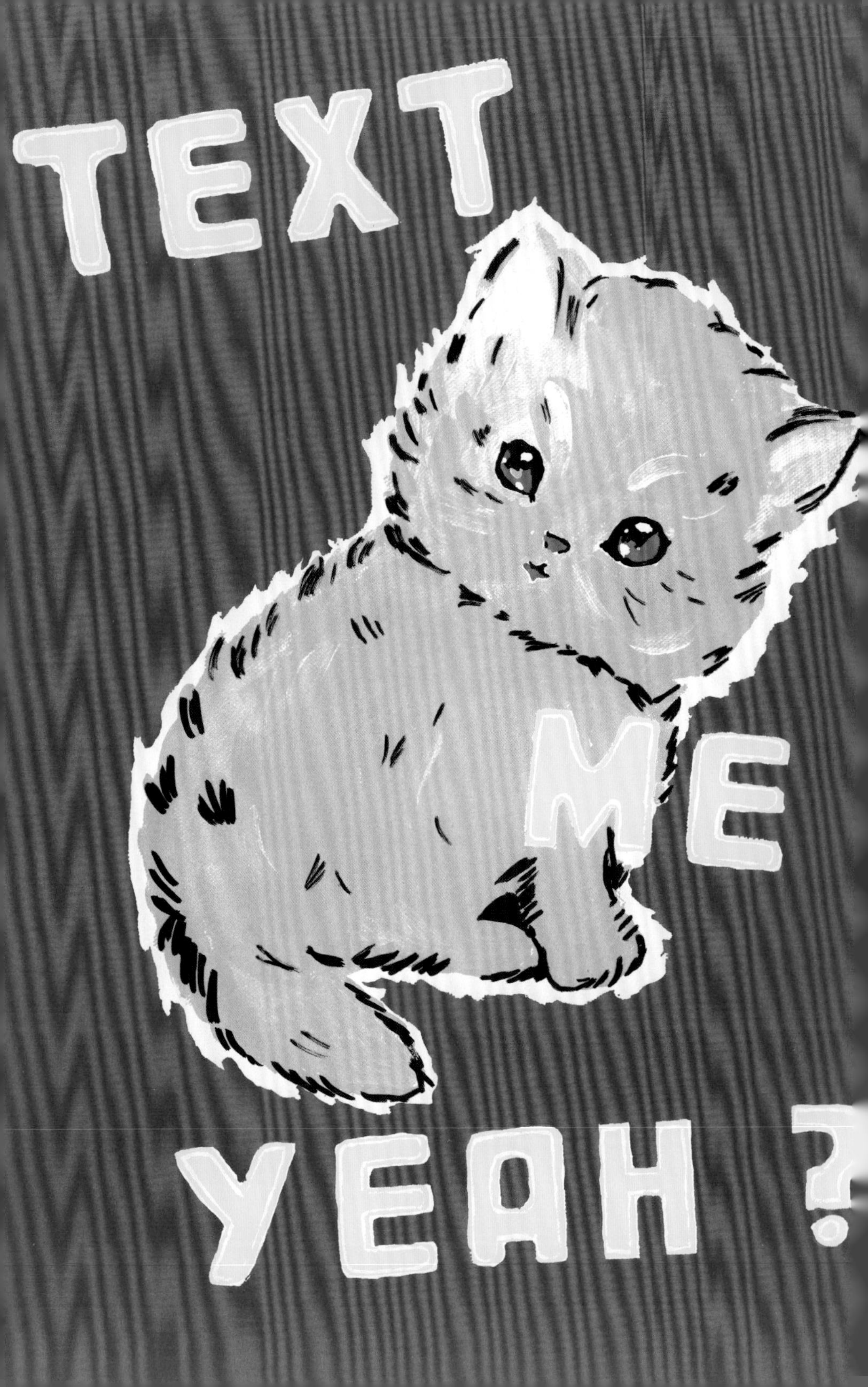
TEXT
ME
YEAH ?

No, no, no you don't
Not a-fucking-gain
With your rhyme and your reason
And your cause

SHEPHERD?
You want to be a shepherd?
Well good for you
Go ahead, your life won't be so tepid

But when it comes around
We barely scream or shout
And rarely am I there
And neither of us care

'Cause I, I, I, I, I guess
we was born to fail
I, I, I, I, I guess we
was born to fail

Yak yak, heart attack
Sat in a taxi all clad in black
Yak yak, heart attack
Sat in a taxi all clad in black
I, I, I, I, I never lie easy
Work with a migrant crew
I work in a menagerie
I don't give a fuck about me or you
'Cause I'm so cold
I'm so cold I'm so cold I'm so cold

'Cause I, I, I, I, I guess we was born to fail
I, I, I, I, I guess we was born to fail
I, I, I, I, I
I, I, I, I, I
Oh no, no, no, no
I, I, I, I, I
Yes, no
Yes, no, yes, no

Faith in

the City

05

MY CAREER MAKES ME FEEL SICK

I got a job in the city

1,   2,   3,   4

There's no god in the city

Uncle Noel's
got cancer
in his brain
Uncle Noel's
got cancer
in his lungs
and his brain
I thought it
would tear
that man apart
Luckily,
uncle Noel's
got Jesus
in his heart

I'm an Aquarius

1, 2, 3, 4

Praise the lord
Praise the lord
Praise the lord
Praise the lord

There's no jobs in the city

Mike lost
116 months
Allegedly all
because of
Benedictine
monks
Bucky
couldn't
help him
find a job
Luckily
Mikey found
himself
at peace
with god

I'm evangelical

1, 2, 3, 4

Praise the lord
(Praise the lord)

Praise the lord
(Praise the lord)

Praise the lord
(Praise the lord)

Praise the lord
(Praise the lord)

Praise the lord
(Praise the lord)

Praise the lord
(Praise the lord)

Praise the lord
(Praise the lord)

Praise the lord
(Praise the lord)

Gotho

My friend is so depressed
He wishes he was dead
I swam inside his head
And this is what he said

Help me, help me
Won't someone
set me free?
There's no right side
of the bed
With a body like mine
and a mind like mine

baby aliens

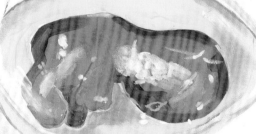

TRAPPED · BY

SELFISH

man !

WORLD'S SADDEST DOG

they say he was

CRYING.

My friend is so depressed
She wanted to have sex
I pissed in the kitchen sink
As she slowly undressed

No way, no way
We never shall decay
We won't last
five fucking minutes
With a body like mine
and a mind like mine

I guess this is as far as she goes
I guess this is as far as we go
I guess this is as far as we go
I guess this is as far

My friend is so depressed
He wishes he was dead
I swam inside his head
And this is what he said

Help me, help me
Won't someone
help me sleep?
There's no right
side of the bed
With a body like mine
and a mind like mine

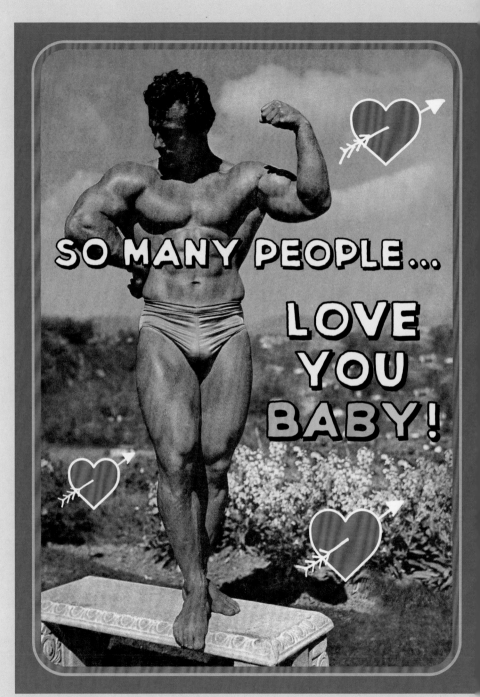

My friend is so depressed
She wanted to have sex
I pissed in the kitchen sink
As she slowly undressed

No way, no way
We never shall decay
We won't last five
fucking minutes
With a body like mine
and a mind like mine

I guess this is as far as we go
I guess this is as far as we go
I guess this is as far as we go
I guess this is as far as we go
I guess this is as far as we go
I guess this is as far as we go

yeah, yeah, yeah, yeah
yeah, yeah, yeah, yeah
yeah, yeah, yeah, yeah
yeah, yeah, yeah, yeah

I guess this is as far as we go
I guess this is as far as we go

My friend is so depressed
My friend is so depresse

Divide &

Conquer 07

Ha, ha

Divide

Ha, ha

Divide

Ha, ha

Divide & conquer

Ha, ha

A loved one perished at the hand
of the barren-hearted right

Divide

A loved one perished at the hand
of the barren-hearted right

Divide

A loved one perished at the hand
of the barren-hearted right

Divide & conquer

Ay   ay   ay   ay   ay

Ay   ayaya   yay

Ay ay aya ay ay

Ayay   aya   yay

A y a y a y a y a y a y

Rachel

Khoo

08

No tax, breaking backs
You ain't their problem
if you're not paying tax
Run it over, be cool
You ain't their problem
if you never
went to school
I'm shaking fast

Whip crack
Whip crack

They don't care about
the summertime
Cheap drugs
and expensive wine
They don't care about
the summertime
Cheap drugs and dear dear wine

Rachel Khoo
Rachel Khoo

Let's drink to the summertime
until we turn blue
I'll tear down every wall
of a C.A.R.A.V.A.G.G.I.O
Just for you
It's true
It's true

Whip Whip crack
Whip crack crack

They don't care about
the summertime
Cheap drugs
and expensive wine
They don't care about
the summertime
Dear drugs and cheap cheap wine
Let's go

My old man's a dustman
He's a sculptor by his trade
He always wears the trousers
And he carves with a hearty spade
We're sinking fast

Whip crack Whip crack

Whip crack

Whip crack

Whip crack

They don't care about
the summertime
Cheap drugs and
expensive wine
They don't care about
the summertime
Cheap drugs and
good ol' good ol' wine

Rachel Khoo

Rachel Khoo

Rachel Khoo

Rachel Khoo

Rachel Khoo

Rachel Khoo

Rachel Khoo

Rachel Khoo

Rachel Khoo

Rachel Khoo

Stendhal

Syndrome 09

Did you see that painting
what Rothko did?

Looks like it was painted
by a two year old kid

SHUT

IT

Ignorance is bliss, yeah?
Well I'm not pleased

Because you spread your opinion
like a rectal disease

HOT AIR

IDLES × Magda Archer

HOT AI

Did you see that photo
what Bellingham took?

He needs to take a leaf
out the screensaver book

If all photos were
as you wanted them to be

There would be page three
as far as the eye could see

HOT AIR

IDLES × Magda Archer

HOT AI

Forgive me you sound stupid
Here lies the one I love
Forgive me you sound stupid
Here lies the one I love

Did you see that selfie
what Francis Bacon did?

Don't look nothing like him –
what a fucking div

HOT AI

Did you see that painting
what Basquiat done?

Looks like it was drawn by
my four year old son

HOT AI

Forgive me you sound stupid
Here lies the one I love
Forgive me you sound stupid
Here lies the one I love

Here he is somehow
Oh, here he is somehow

Exeter

10

Na Na Na Na Na Na Na Na Na Nothing ever happer

It seems like no one cares
I think I'll take the stairs
'Cause nothing ever

He punched himself in the
face to prove he wasn't gay
'Cause nothing ever happens

Over and over and over
and over again

Na Na Na Na Na Na Na Na Na Nothing ever

I dropped onto my knees
And prayed to Jesus, please
Will something fucking
happen

Then they killed
poor George dead

They put a hammer
through his head
Now nothing ever happens

Over and over and over
and over again

Na Na Na Na Na Na Na Na Na Nothing ever happer

IDLES × Magda Archer

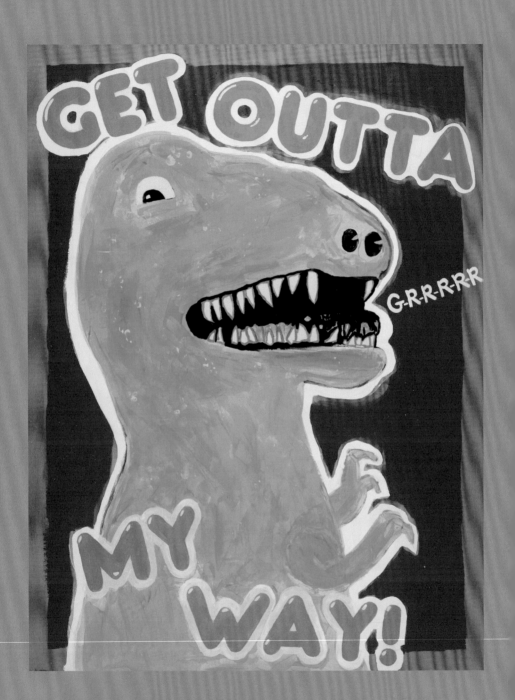

Steven's	in the bar for a bar fight
Nick's	in the bar for a bar fight
Danny's	in the bar for a bar fight
Grant's	in the bar for a bar fight
Scott's	in the bar for a bar fight
Shit-eyes	in the bar for a bar fight
John Gerrard's	in the bar for a bar fight
Charlie's	in the bar for a bar fight
Andy's	in the bar for a bar fight
Stewart's	in the bar for a bar fight
Gareth's	in the bar for a bar fight
Pimmy's	in the bar for a bar fight
Cranky's	in the bar for a bar fight
Heather's	in the bar for a bar fight
Biker's	in the bar for a bar fight

Over and over and over and over again
Nothing ever happens

Benzocaine 11

Ha   ha   ha
Ha   ha   ha

Oh Benzocaine
        I think it's a crime
                    Ha   ha   ha

        The way you look in your baby's eyes
        You won't see mine
        You won't see mine
                    Ha   ha   ha
                    Ha   ha   ha

                            The memories will stay
The brain will start to fade
Boredom creeps in jade

With God on Benzocaine

Oh Benzocaine
Oh Benzocaine
Oh Benzocaine
Oh Benzocaine

Ha   ha   ha

Ha   ha   ha

Oh Benzocaine

Chalk white
Gobshite

Bleeding gums

I thought the Benzocaine

was supposed to numb

supposed to numb

supposed to numb

supposed to numb

supposed to numb

Oh Benzocaine

Oh Benzocaine

Oh Benzocaine

Oh Benzocaine

White

Privilege

12

BE LUCKY

How many optimists does it take

to change a lightbulb?

None!

Their butler changes the lightbulb

Always poor Never bored

The S.L.C.
want
Timmy's
student loan
back

He'd

happily
oblige
but
he's u s e d it all

on
g   a   k

Always poor Never bored

One miscarriage
Two abortions
One degree
Seven jobs
Sally danced her socks off
As Jesus sobbed

Always poor Never bored

I couldn't dance with your mother
'Cause she passed out on your stairs

Always poor N

Swing batter, batter, batter
Swing batter, batter, batter
Swing batter, batter, batter
Swing

Compensate with humour
or if really bored then sing

Always poor N

Always p

r bored

Swing batter, batter, batter
Swing batter, batter, batter
Swing batter, batter, batter
Swing

Compensate with humour
or if really bored then sing

r bored

or Never borec

Yeah, dance 'til the sun goes round Yeah, dance 'til the sun goes round Yeah, dance 'til the sun goes round Yeah, dance 'til the sun goes round Yeah, dance 'til the sun goes round Yeah, dance 'til the sun goes round Yeah, dance 'til the sun goes round Yeah, dance 'til the sun goes round Yeah, dance 'til the sun goes round Yeah, dance 'til the sun goes round Yeah, dance 'til the sun goes round Yeah, dance 'til the sun goes round Yeah, dance 'til the sun goes round Yeah, dance 'til the sun goes round Yeah, dance 'til the sun goes round

IDLES × Magda Archer

Slow

Savage 13

I'm

sorry

for

not being

the person

you want me

to be

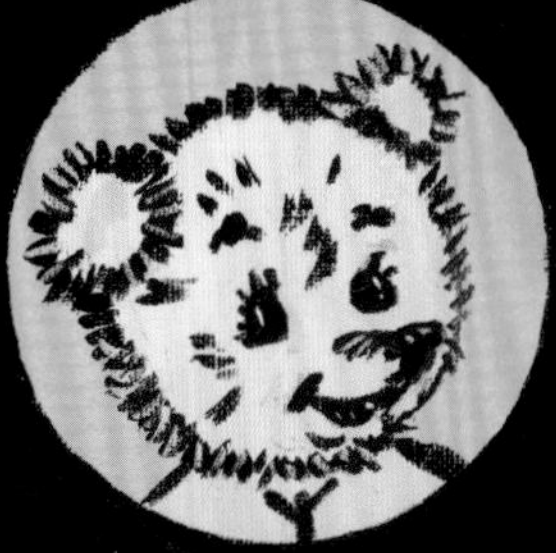

It was dark and
cold as a knife when
we tussled through
the pines

You can howl at
the bedsheets

Scream at the moon
if you like

But it won't help   But it might help
me some, won't   me some, might help
help me if we die   me if you cry

                                    She said, 'Wait! We'll
                                    be better if we wait,
                                    better if we wait.'

I said, 'There's no amount
of time to carry the weight.'

                    La   da   da

'Cause I'm the worst
lover you've ever had

I'm the worst lover you'll ever have

For two years   For two years in
in a row I forgot   a row I thought it
your birthday   was a Thursday

Maybe it was God

Maybe it was coke

Maybe I'm a drunk

I don't know

But at least now
I remember your birthday

ALL YOU CAN

LOSE IS

EVERY

THING.

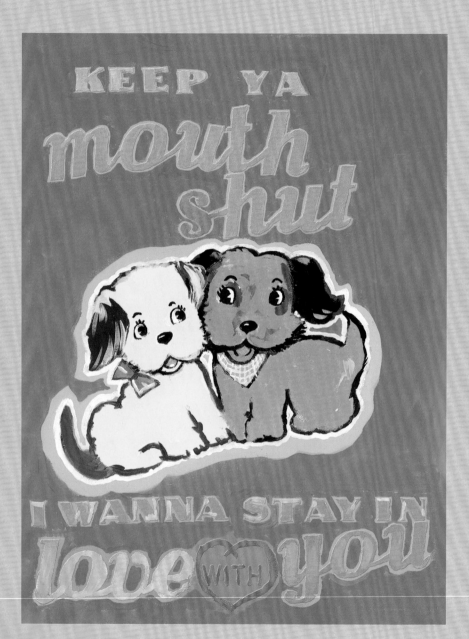

Cause I'm the worst lover
you'll ever have

Hands down goddamn
worst lover
you'll ever have

La   da   da

Cause I'm the worst lover
you'll ever have

I'm the worst lover
you'll ever have

I remember when I was six, in a new class and sitting next to my friend Jimmy. He laughed when I drew cartoons all over my exercise book – I thought the teacher had said to decorate it but, as it turned out, I'd got it wrong. She had just told us to write our names on the covers. Jimmy called everyone over to see my book and laugh. Now I think to myself, just make what you make and don't hang around to hear whether you 'got it wrong' – just keep moving, keep making.

This book was on, then it was off... then, once it was ON again, it seemed to have acquired a little 'ready brek glow' – it resonated, it felt special. That feeling grew and the book kept making me stop and think – about Joe's lyrics, about all the juxtapositions, the people, the relationships and the connections between the pictures and the words... ALL of it. And speaking of connections, I think IDLES and I are like two twinned towns. It was a question of 'hang on, wait a minute, what have THEY got in common?' But then the realisation, 'OH, I see, oh yes, I get it... Of course... Put the sign up!'

In a world where people are dropped or replaced so easily – thank you, Joe, for saying you'd only do this if I did...

Thanks too to Evie Tarr, Leo Field and Nick Linford. We couldn't have done it without you.

Magda Archer

Joe Talbot is is the lead vocalist and lyricist for British rock band IDLES. Originally from Newport, Wales, Talbot moved to Bristol to study, where he formed the band in 2009 along with Adam Devonshire (bass), Jon Beavis (drums), Lee Kiernan and Mark Bowen (guitar).

Magda Archer is a London-based artist. Her work has been widely exhibited and she has collaborated with major fashion designers including Marc Jacobs, Comme des Garçons and Jenny Packham. Her public posters for flyingleaps have become iconic features of London's cityscape.

On the cover: 'Good Boy' by Magda Archer

First published in the United Kingdom in 2023 by Volume
This edition published in the United Kingdom in 2024 by
Thames & Hudson Ltd, 181A High Holborn, London WC1V 7QX

IDLES x Magda Archer Brutalism: *Illustrated Lyrics* © 2023 Volume
Foreword © 2023 Joe Talbot
Lyrics © 2023 Joe Talbot, Kobalt Music Publishing/Hal Leonard Licensing
Artworks © 2023 Magda Archer

Illustrated Lyrics series concept by Evie Tarr
Layout designed by Leo Field

Created in collaboration with London- and Brighton-based company FORM Presents. FORM are a group of passionate music fans who work with an incredible range of artists on their live careers in the UK, from grassroots venues to arena shows, while also facilitating and producing a range of other work in music and the arts.

British Library Cataloguing-in-Publication Data
A catalogue record for this book is available from the British Library

Library of Congress Control Number 2023935364

ISBN 978-0-500-02697-7

Printed in China by RR Donnelley

MIX
Paper | Supporting responsible forestry
FSC
www.fsc.org
FSC® C144853

Be the first to know about our new releases, exclusive content and author events by visiting
thamesandhudson.com
thamesandhudsonusa.com
thamesandhudson.com.au